Natural Supplement For Extra Man Power Booster

Boost your testosterone & libido level, sexual desire or urge, self-confidence, penis size, bone and repair damage tissues, burn excess fat, and stabilize high blood pressure with the best natural supplement.

Dr. Walker Sax

Contents

CHAPTER FIVE 29

Natural Supplement For Extra Man Power Booster
Copyright Notice. By Dr. Walker Sax

Introduction

Have you been thinking of how to get a 100% natural testosterone enhancer and men's extra power pills or supplement that will be able to prevent and treat you from any kind of erectile dysfunctions, increase your testosterone level, enrich your bones health, minimize your blood sugar rate, burn down your surplus body fat (pot belly) enhance your energy, stamina, enlarge your penis and improve your sexual urge or desire to enjoy a long lasting erection with a longer, harder and tougher erection?

If you really desire it, you don't have to worry anymore for its never too late for there are a lots of natural enhancement supplement with the most finest 100% natural ingredients constituent together to treat and also keep you completely free from erectile dysfunctions forever out there for your extra man power to keep you energetic and ever ready for your sexual session with your partner.

CHAPTER ONE
What Does Testosterone Mean?

Testosterone is the most vital sex hormones in male and have the main effect in men functionalities. And belong to a men classes of hormones referred to as Androgens which can equally be indicated to as steroids.

The testicles is where the productions of the testosterone is carry out and later the mind nerve area and pituitary organ regulate the preparations. Irregular condition of testosterone in the body is the mechanism that recognize the enhancement of men conceptive tissues, for instance, prostate & tastes, grows the mass, lengthens voice, thick facial hair and furthermore. Youths in their twenties are mainly in their testosterone production major and it is substantial in male as it is vital for distinctive sperm generation, entire success and health.

Natural Supplement For Extra Man Power Booster

Researchers has started that testosterone is allied with men behavior or conduct, feelings or sentiments, psychological or physical ability, dislike and mood.

What Are The Elementary Function Of Testosterone?

The basics of testosterone in the body are:

i.   It helps to minimize excess body and midsection fat

ii.   Its aids the formation of sperm

iii.   Its aids growth of body hair

iv.   Its boost the thickness of bone and quality

v.   It enhance maturity quickly

vi.   It boost sex or assist moxie

vii.   Adequate energy to function well at the rec area

viii.   It boost your confidence

ix.   It rise your strength level

x.   It aids the prevention of osteoporosis

xi.   It aids the growth of the sex organ

What Is Poor (Low) Testosterone Level In Male?

Low testosterone which can also be referred as testosterone insufficiency disorder (TD) is the level at which gonads or testicles can't be able to produce adequate testosterone needed in the body and this may be as a result of some medical problem. Research study that was carry out on testosterone establish the facts that from the age of 30 a man testosterone begin to decline by 1% and this might on the other hand speedy a reduction in both physical health and entire prosperity.

As showed by the American urology Association (AUA) low testosterone is acknowledged when the blood testosterone level is below 300 Nanograms for each deciliter (ng/dl).

What Regularly Occurs When Your Testosterone Level Is Low?

When the men testosterone is poor or low it may trigger the associated disorder which include:

i. Trouble resting

ii. Shriveled testicle

iii. It might prompt to poor memory

iv. Weak erection

v. You will be subjected to low sperm check

vi. You will be subjected to low sex request (moxie)

vii. You will be subjected to erectile dysfunctions (ED)

viii. You might be prompt to bones weakness

ix. You will be subjected to low stamina and endurance level to stay longer in your sexual session

x. Inadequate   vivacity to perform better in the rec

Natural Supplement For Extra Man Power Booster

center

xi.   Fatigue

xii.   Having hot flashes

xiii.   Absence of fixation

xiv.   Increase in surplus weight and midsection fat

xv.   Subjected to hair loss

xvi.   Lean bulk

What Can Cause Decrease Of Testosterone Level?

Male are most likely going to develop low testosterone from the associated condition such as:

i.   Absence of sufficient component such as Vitamin D, Zinc etc.

ii.   Chemotherapy session

iii.   Symptoms of infection

iv.   Klinefelter disease

v.   Symptoms like HIV/AIDS

vi.   Prader-willi ailment

vii.   Symptoms of liver or kidney disorder

viii.   Sometimes low testosterone level can be as a result of age grade

ix.   Pituitary organ disorder

x.   And also when the gonad is not in good health (herm)

CHAPTER TWO
The Importance Of Natural Testosterone Booster
What Is Natural Supplement For Extra Man Power Booster?

'Natural Supplement For Extra Man Power Booster" is a natural men's testosterone booster that is made for the purpose of boosting testosterone level, build muscle, burn surplus body fat, increase your energy, stamina and endurance level, enhance strong bones, minimize blood pressure, decrease muscle fatigue, boost mood, improve sexual stimulus or urge and also enhance cognitive and concentrative functionalities.

What Are the Advantages of Natural Supplement For Extra Man Power Booster?

The advantages of Natural Supplement for Extra Man Power Booster are:

i.   100% Testosterone Booster aids the energy drive in male to fully satisfy their partners during their

Natural Supplement For Extra Man Power Booster

sexual session in other words keep them energetic and ever ready.

ii.   100% Natural Testosterone Booster increases bulk and lean muscle in weight lifters.

iii.   This supplement aids the production of testosterone in a simple and safe manner

iv.   It enhanced both physical and mental performance

v.   100% Natural Testosterone Booster aid vivacity level and physical quality, this will enable you to be excessively self-motivated during exercise

vi.   100% Natural Testosterone Booster aid with enlightening your state of mind and lessening pressure

vii.   It inspires you to recuperate your control in the rec center

viii.   100% Natural Testosterone Booster causes you to be driven and balanced, making you to be progressively more optimistic at work

ix.   It inspires you to recuperate your control in the rec center

Natural Supplement For Extra Man Power Booster

x.	100% Natural Testosterone Booster aids to weakened down muscle versus fat mainly around the waist, it equally decay cholesterol level

What Are The Possible Benefits of 100% Natural Testosterone Booster?

The benefits of 100% Natural Testosterone Booster include:

i.	This supplement come along with a guarantee of money price cut if after 60 days of consumption and you are not satisfy with the anticipated result.

ii.	The manufacturer of Teso Fuel Natural Testosterone Booster clearly document all the fixing and the sum of servings make use of on the name

iii.	This supplement is a distinctive testosterone booster made from the finest mineral and herbs

iv.	This superb booster can be ship globally and shipment is absolutely free

v.	100% Natural Testosterone Booster doesn't necessarily need a profession solution since it is locally grown medication that is not made of any fixing which require remedy

vi.   It aids your skin making it to glow and look ever more youthful

vii.   Even at some point you stop taking this superb supplement your enhanced testosterone level will still remain the same and won't drop.

viii. When you begin to administer this supplement you don't need to change your regular eating habit

ix.   This supplement is available in more than 80 diverse nation around the globe.

Note: It has an enormous amount of positive audit on the web

What Are The Disadvantages of Natural Supplement Extra Man Power Booster?

The disadvantage of 100% Natural Testosterone Booster include:

i.   It is very expensive

ii.   It may Sometime take longer effort to get expected result because of the different body system

iii.   It can't be reachable for those who don't have access to the internet as it can only be obtainable from the manufacturer site

CHAPTER THREE

How Does Natural Supplement For Extra Man Power Booster Works?

100% Natural Testosterone Booster works in realizing three (3) vital elements that is known with thorough testosterone creation. These three constituents are:

1. luteinizing Hormone Also Referred To As "LH"

2. Sex Hormones Binding Globulin Molecules Also Referred To As "SHBG"

3. And lastly, Female Hormones Also Referred To As "Estrogen & Prolactin"

We should take a gander at these three (3) elements essentially:

i.   Luteinizing hormone (HH): the boosting source of 100% Natural Testosterone Booster is (D-AA-CC) this fixing is completely 100% common

Natural Supplement For Extra Man Power Booster

amino corrosive that helps in flagging the cerebrum (nerve center) to transport the needed luteinizing hormone (LH) in the body structure and Zinc is equally another fixing that is used to really attractive form of this amazing supplement that helps in improving the pituitary organ to release luteinizing hormone (LH). Research taken in regards of Luteinizing Hormone (LH) have establish the fact that this hormone aids in intensifying the level at which your testis produces testosterone through a regular of 42% in twelve days.

ii. Secondly is the Sex Hormone Binding Globulin Molecules also referred to as (SHBG): the SHBG element that is present in the body is the mechanism that makes the testosterone to be

Natural Supplement For Extra Man Power Booster

naturally dormant. Even with the knowledge tha

the atom can do, the manufacturer of 100%

Natural Testosterone Booster, certify fixing suc

as: vex root and magnesium are integrated into th

making of this superb supplement. How does thi

fixing work? All things put in place, the root aid

in constraining together with the SHBG atom i

other to ensure that all the natural activ

testosterone are responsively made obtainable fc

the body structure. Currently, the magnesium aid

in lessening the extent of SHBG particles that i

present in the circulatory system. This is nc

entirely control as (Boron) is equally anothe

fascinating fixing used that is really taking shap

of this superb supplement to reduce the bloo

extents of SHBG which in return will speedy

Natural Supplement For Extra Man Power Booster

boost on your testosterone level.

iii. Lastly, Estrogen and Prolactin: is a women sexual hormone that is present in an instant extent in each men's body. The availabilities of surplus estrogen and prolactin in the body structure can reduce your testosterone level. This is the actual inspiration behind the reason why 100% Natural Testosterone Booster is formed with some carefully selected fixing such as: (Boron, Nettle Leaf Extract and Fenugreek) to regulate estrogen and prolactin rate in men's body structure. Researchers has establish the facts, which boron can aid to lessening the aspect of estrogen by 39% within the period of 7 days in men's body structure. Concentrate furthermore reveals that Nettle Leaf Extract can equally aid in reducing the estrogen amount on men and boost testosterone level. In addition, the use of Fenugreek also aids in lessening the aspect of prolactin.

Why Do I Need 100% Natural Testosterone Booster?

In reality, as a teenager in your youthful age, your testosterone production level will rise until you have attain the age of 30. At this level or year, you will be energetic, plus more beneficiary, one hundred percent openly active, negligence and self-confidence, form slender muscle, gain crisp and healthy hair growth, more grounded bones and solid heart. Currently, attaining the age of 30, your testosterone rate will begin to diminish by 1% annually, at the time you get to 80, there is a probability that you are more likely than not began disposition: a weak sex drive, glucose problem (diabetes), feeling weak, muscle injury maybe troubled, put up surplus weight, generate more

Natural Supplement For Extra Man Power Booster
fragile and tinny bones also cardiovascular problem.

However, with the making of 100% Natural Testosterone Booster, you are guarantee of coming out of your previous misery lifestyle, regaining your confidence, intensify your sexual inclination, gain more grounded bones, more healthy heart, regularly burning, boost disposition, and shed surplus fat and produce suitable muscle with a remarkable component with a gigantic boost on your vivacity, endurance and stamina to rise performance at your peak.

Who 100% Natural Testosterone Booster Prepared For?

This superb supplement is made for the purpose of the following individuals:

i.   If you have attain the age of 30 and you desire to boost or support your testosterone level

ii.   It for any man that has attain the age of 18 and

desire to restore his self-confidence

iii. For weight lifters and competitors who desire to boost up their pace during their work-out session

iv. For men who desperate want to burn down surplus body and midsection fat

v. It for individual who are seriously craving for six pack and want to build it

vi. It for individual who have attain the age of 18 that desire to support their sex drive

vii. For any individual who have attain the age of 18 that is anticipating to aid his bulk

viii. It is actually made for men for desire adequate vivacity, stamina and endurance to maximize their performance in bed

ix. It is made for men looking for a distinctive testosterone developer with no side effects or

Natural Supplement For Extra Man Power Booster

hazard.

CHAPTER FOUR
What Are The Dosage of 100% Natural Testosterone Booster?

Each 100% Natural Testosterone Booster container carries 120 supplement which is supposed to last you for 30 days. You are recommended to ingest 4 supplement daily. You are to ingest it approximately 20 minute before breakfast. You also note that with or without working out you are supposed to take 4 supplement for each day. As you continue to consume the exact recommended dosage regularly, you will begin to experience an enhancement for your disposition fixation, sex urge and pulse within one to three weeks of using the supplement however for reduction in fat and cholesterol, muscle development, aid quality and vivacity you will have to continue using the supplement as recommended for a period of four to seven weeks.

Furthermore, you should note that you don't really need a

Natural Supplement For Extra Man Power Booster professional's remedy hence the medication is completely natural without any medicine fixing.

What Are The Safety Measure for Consuming 100% Natural Testosterone Booster?

The safety measures of consuming 100% Natural Testosterone Booster include:

i. You can't consume this supplement if you are below 18 years old

ii. Women are not allowed to consume this supplement

iii. Please this supplement should be kept safely out of the reach of children below the age of 18

iv. Please ensure that you consult your physician if you are having any medical disorder before you start using this supplement

v.   Don't take more than the recommended dosage daily

vi.   If you are sensitive to any of the ingredients included in the making of this superb supplement please you should consult a medical specialist before you can start consuming it.

What Are the Possible Side Effects I Can Experience from Using 100% Natural Testosterone Booster?

Though, this supplement is not known with any possible reactions, however overdose of this supplement might lead to the following symptoms:

i.   Fatigue

ii.   Vomiting

iii.   Headache

iv.   Stomach pain and

v.   Nausea

CHAPTER FIVE
The Complete Ingredients Of Natural Supplement For Extra Man Power Booster

The following are the constituent ingredients use for the

making of this superb supplement:

i.   Red Ginseng Extract

ii.   Nettle Leaf Extract

iii.   D-Aspartic Acid

iv.   Zinc

v.   Magnesium

vi.   Vitamin B6

vii.   Vitamin D3

viii.   Boron

ix.   Bioperine

What is Red Ginseng Extract?

Red Ginseng also referred to as panax ginseng which is well

known for its remarkable recovering properties. It is

Natural Supplement For Extra Man Power Booster discover in the mountain of Eastern Asia and belong to the family of Araliaceae. This plant is growth largely for its essentials fundamentals hence the root is the source of Ginseng and that is the area the huge bulk of the nutrient, different minerals that helps medically and health are settled. This particular type of ginseng is use as a vital ingredient in this supplement since it form more than double the quality of other ginseng specie. Consumers of the Red Panax ginseng largely look for a long period developed certified ginseng substances, because the more seasoned ginseng often carries more remarkable recovering effects that the newly developed ones.

The Red Panex ginseng developed establish the fact that it carries more higher quality substance and more effective for it useful wellbeing because it is usually thicker and full with supplement. Researchers reveals that this unique root is

Natural Supplement For Extra Man Power Booster measure as one of the finest vital herbs for enhancing Testosterone.

The advantage of Red Ginseng includes:

i. Ginseng helps to support vivacity quality and endurance

ii. Ginseng helps to strengthen the resistance structure

iii. It increase the advents of luteinizing hormone, this stimulate testosterone release

iv. Ginseng helps to improve the aspect of nitric corrosive in the blood, this will enlarge the bulk

v. Ginseng helps you to thrash surplus muscle to fat rate

vi. It helps to repair high cholesterol

vii. Ginseng also helps to support your psychological and physical wellbeing

viii.   Ginseng helps to improve your psychological ability and state of mind

ix.   Ginseng helps to support moxie, making your sexual session more enjoyable and pleasant

What is Nettle leaf Extract?

Nettle Leaf Extract which can also be referred to as Stinging bramble or Urtica dioica is a flourishing plant that belong to a family known as Urticaceae and can be located around the globe. The leaf has pretty hair around it which when touch will release a stinging sensation. It has a history that has been long use for the making of traditional medication, tea materials and even food. Researchers has establish the facts that when the testosterone bound with the sex hormone denying globulin (SHBG) it will reduce the testosterone useless in men's body, in view of that, when Nettle Leaf is consumed, the lignans properties that is found in it wil

Natural Supplement For Extra Man Power Booster

imbroglio with the SHBG to revoke the threat to testosterone, in this manner it enable the body to make use of the testosterone available for now. It equally aid to restrict the change of testosterone into Dihydrotestosterone (DHT), this will reduce the side effects connected to prostate disease in male.

The advantage of Nettle Leaf Extract includes:

i. Nettle Leaf can be used to treat skin infection, skin break out and blemishes

ii. Nettle Leaf forestall baldness in male

iii. It can be used to treat muscle irritation cause by stress

iv. It can be used to protect the cell firm and DNA from injuries

v. It can be used to stimulate moxie in male

vi. It can be used to reduce surplus fat from the body

vii.   It aids the treatment of insufficient iron

viii.   It can be used to calm distress in the body

ix.   It is used to support testosterone, this means more maleness, less instant fat and more fixation

x.   It works as an opposite of weakness and increase your physical performance

xi.   Nettle Leaf can also be used to treat asthma, feed fever, hack and sensitivity

What is Fenugreek Extract?

Fenugreek as well referred to as Trigonella foenum-graecum is a multi-reason Pl0ant that is growth for the two leaves and seed and it belong to a family known as Fabaceae. This remarkable herbs that can be discover in the western Asia, Mediterran and some places in Africa for a particular period of time now has been in used to treat some sicknesses, boost nutrient, for skin nourishment, boost endurance and increase health. Researchers carry out some studies on Fenugreek concentrate establish the facts that it helps drive in male, burn down fat, support testosterone level and boost bulk. This is actual the main reason why this ingredient is included I the making of this supplement 100% Natural Testosterone Booster.

The advantage of fenugreek concentrate includes:

i. Fenugreek can be used to lighten temperament

ii. Fenugreek can be used to get rid of muscle irritation

iii. It can be used to shuns erectile brokenness

iv. Fenugreek can be used to increase your entire sexual performance

v. Fenugreek can be used to boost insulin release which can build bulk in your body in the waken of formulating

vi.   It can be used to boost sex urge, strength and allure in male

vii.   Fenugreek enrich your kidney and liver health

viii.   It aids simple integration

ix.   Fenugreek aids the production of testosterone level

Furthermore, the symptoms of ingesting surplus of Fenugreek concentration includes:

i.   You may experience constipation

ii.   Frequent urinating

iii.   Diarrhea

iv.   Nausea

v.   Too much sweating

What is D-Aspartic Acid?

D-Aspartic corrosive is a usually happening amino corrosive this is used in the biosynthesis of proteins. It

Natural Supplement For Extra Man Power Booster

groups in certain tissues known as testicles and pituitary organ where it try to stimulate the coming of hormone, for instance, testosterone, progesterone, increase hormone and many more this insignificant amino corrosive can be generally formed by the body from the use of nourishment such as: dairy, milks, chicken, fish, meat, almonds, nuts, vegetable, grains and many more. Research reveals that it aid the testosterone level, increase muscle and vivacity.

The advantage of D-Aspartic Acid includes:

i.   It helps to minimize hypertension

ii.   It helps to regulate the body hormone

iii.   It helps to boost the nature of sperm

iv.   It helps to support testosterone level

v.   It can be used to help the enhancement of muscle development and athletic performance

vi.   it serve as a support for moxie and sexual

Natural Supplement For Extra Man Power Booster

satisfaction

vii.   it can be used to increase the function of the

cerebrum

viii.   it can be used to enhance muscle development and

repairs

Note: excess consumption of D-Aspartic Acid in the body

can lead to the following side effects:

i.   it might lead to unwanted effect on blood

cholesterol kidney and liver problem

ii.   can prompt to vomiting

iii.   headache

iv.   stomach upset

What Is Zinc?

Zinc which is the key element in the twelve gathering of the

recurrent table is a vital element needed in the body for a

better life and unaffected structure. It can't be provided by

Natural Supplement For Extra Man Power Booster

our bodies and lack of sufficient zinc in the body might result to illness. This substantial element take responsibility of few functions in the body, for instance, stimulating the drive of 100 distinctive substances in the body, insusceptible bulk, consumes supplements, DNA and protein generation, restores wounds speedily. It also builds the production of testosterone in male and prevent the probabilities of erectile disorder.

What are the possible side effects Zinc deficiency?

Lack of adequate admission of Zinc might lead to the following side effects:

    i.   Having a symptoms of skin infection

    ii.   Wound might take a longer time before recovering

    iii.   You might be having problem associated with circulation

    iv.   Having hair loss for both male and female

v.   Having a weak structure

vi.   You are prompt to poor vision

vii.   Harm of craving

viii.   Having a poor feeling of smell

ix.   Issues with absorption

What types of food are very rich in Zinc?

These diets when included to your consumption routine can build the quantity of Zinc in your body. They includes:

i.   Peas

ii.   Lobster and crab

iii.   Beefs

iv.   Baked beans

v.   Oyster

vi.   Pumpkin seeds

vii.   Bean

viii.   Peanut

Natural Supplement For Extra Man Power Booster

ix.   Yoghurt

x.   Pork midsection etc.

Zinc has the following advantage. These include:

i.   The ingestion of adequate Zinc in the body helps you to gain more stamina and endurance level during your sexual session with your partner

ii.   It helps the nourishment of skin

iii.   It support the enhancement of testosterone level in the body

iv.   It helps to reduce hypertension level in human body

v.   It helps to eradicated the symptoms of unwanted virus in the body

vi.   It enrich your memory ability

vii.   It helps to regulate the body hormone

Lack of sufficient state of Zinc in the body can lead to the

Natural Supplement For Extra Man Power Booster following:

i.   Symptoms of headache

ii.   Stomach pain

iii.   Vomiting

iv.   Allergies

What is Magnesium?

Magnesium is one of the vital supplement or minerals that help the body to stay sound, it is necessary for the paramount working of several substances in the body. It undertakes diverse functions in the body, for instance, regulating nerve and muscles abilities, circulatory anxiety, and glucose level, controlling the state of mind, protein, DNA and improvement of bones wellbeing.

Food that are highly rich in Magnesium are:

i.   Edamame

ii.   Sunflower seed

iii.   Dark chocolate

iv.   Peanut

v.   Black beans

vi.   Whole wheat

vii.   Almond

viii.   Spinach

ix.   Avocados

What is Magnesium inadequacy?

Magnesium inadequacy means poor or low aspect of magnesium in your body or when your body lack adequate magnesium to stay healthy. The side effect of inadequacy of magnesium in your body include:

i.   Having high pulse

ii.   Asthma

iii.   Abnormal heartbeat

iv.   Absence of coordination

v.   Symptoms of seizures

vi.   Tremor

vii.   Lack of appetite

viii.   Muscle spasms

ix.   Nystagums

x.   Poor condition.

The advantage of Magnesium includes:

i.   It control and stabilize hypertension

ii.   It boost you to recover quickly from absurd exercise

iii.   It boost you to obtain quality rest

iv.   It enhances your physical, mental and fervent wellbeing

v.   It boost bulk

vi.   It forestalls bone weakness

vii.   It helps you to gain quality vivacity and stamina

viii.   It improve your mood

ix.   It enhances the flexibility of muscle

x.   It rise the amount of testosterone generation in
your body.

What is Vitamin B6?

Nutrient B6 which can also be referred to as pyridoxine is one the Vitamin B gathering of vital supplements that be originate in diets such as: natural foodstuffs, vegetables, grains and liver. It is needed in the human body to form starch, amino corrosive and fats. Researchers establish the facts that the human body can hardly generate B6 in this manner so you will have to get it from some diet and supplement such as 100% Natural Testosterone Booster. It is necessary for the proper working of the sensory system, insusceptible structure and mind. Magnesium is essentially a testosterone boosting intensifier supplements and

Natural Supplement For Extra Man Power Booster additionally give you adequate vivacity to function better without getting exhausted.

The possible advantages of Vitamin B6 are:

i.   It aids your body to generate white platelets which helps your body to fight against disease

ii.   It neutralize diabetes

iii.   It helps to correct vision

iv.   It helps to correct joint and muscle pain

v.   It helps to enrich memory and personal capability

vi.   It helps to neutralize the danger of coronary sickness

vii.   It boost your body to supply hemoglobin

viii.   It enable protein to repair tissues like muscles

ix.   It helps to nourish the skin and keep it sound.

What is Vitamin D3

Nutrient D3 which is also referred to as Colecalciferol is called the daylight nutrient hence when the rays of the sun touches the skin, the body react over it into Vitamin D. this nutrient that can be seen inside many different kind of dietary supplement and sustenance, for instance, eggs, cod liver, constant milk and fish is beneficial to everyone. It is turn into hormone in the body, in this manner, it is surge in the circulatory system to help withhold calcium and phosphorous that is acquire from processed sustenance source. Calcium is use for the structure of strong bone and bulk and it also undertake a primary function in the development of hormone in your body.

The possible advantages of Vitamin D3 are:

i. It helps to reduce surplus weight

ii. It helps to reinforce or strengthen erectile capacity

iii.   It helps to boost solid prostate

iv.   It helps to enrich your sperm to remain solid

v.   It helps to boost your entire wellbeing

vi.   It helps to enhance a decent and sound physical performance

vii.   It helps to balance or smooth circulatory pressure

viii.   It helps regulate or control the glucose level in your body

ix.   It forestall the level of testosterone varying over into estrogen

x.   It toughen the safe structure and retain muscle quality

Overdose portion can result to:

i.   Absence of focus

ii.   Vomiting

iii.   Having constipation

iv.   Kidney stone

v.   Weakness

What is Boron?

Boron is a very vital mineral that help to develop the entire body system. Lots of terrifying illness such as osteoporosis and joint pain are obviously treated by it. Boron increases the human ability to integrate calcium and magnesium these 2 minerals functions together with Boron to empower your body to feel better. Noble is richly found food such as: avocado, pears, olive, red grape, potato, soybeans, plums, currants, tomato, shelled nut, lentils, spread, kiwis, apples, hazelnuts, onion and oranges.

In any condition, insufficient of boron can result to irregular digestion of magnesium and calcium. This might also prompt to the following disease:

a. Osteoporosis

b. Hyperthyroidism

c. Hyperinsulinemia

d. Neural anomaly

e. Sexual hormone roughness and

f. joint pain

The advantages of Boron include:

i.   Boron helps to keep the gum and teeth healthy

ii.   Boron speedy the recovering of wound

iii.   Boron helps the treatment and corrective action of joint inflammation

iv.   It also helps the bone development edges. In this aspect, boron work related to the hip with calcium to strengthen the bone

v.   Boron helps to reduce the quantity of SHBG in the blood, this will increase the amount of open testosterone obtainable in the body

vi.   Boron also works to elevate embryonic development as it's substantial for reproduction

vii.   It can equally be used to treat malignancy and the improvement of solid protein inhibitors

viii.   It safeguard the body against oxidative stress

ix.   It reduce the allergenic and fiery situation

x.   Boron increases the estrogen levels in the body

What is Bioperine?

Bioperine which is also referred to as Ruler of Flavors is the 1st concentrate discover in Piper nigrum "dark pepper natura product" and it has 95% piperine. This superb herb has long been in used for decades as seasoning, taste for banquet and component for numbers of different conventional medicine and health supplement and general well-being. Research that was carryout on Bioperine establish the facts that Bioperine has been one of the vital

Natural Supplement For Extra Man Power Booster component used largely for numerous treatment recommended around the world. It undertakes the work og a bioavailability booster of different mixtures and supplement in the human body system. This is actually the main reason why this ingredient is added in the making of this superb supplement.

The advantages of Bioperine include:

i.   It stimulate digestion

ii.   It helps to burn down surplus body fat

iii.   It helps to enrich human memory

iv.   It helps to boost the development of blood in the whole body

v.   It helps to lessen stress, sadness, weakness and tension

vi.   It helps to counteract irritations in the human body

vii.   It often used to prevent the risk of coronary sickness

viii.   It helps to minimize the symptoms of hypertension kind of Asthma

ix.   It also serve as aid for easy digestion and treat stomach related problem in the body

x.   It helps to boost the body to hold all the component used in the making of 100% Natural Testosterone Booster

xi.   Another substantial advantage of Bioperine is the improvement of tough structure to fight against any type of ailment

Excessive consumption of Bioperine may possibly prompt:

Natural Supplement For Extra Man Power Booster

i.   Nausea

ii.   Stomach disorder

iii.   It can prompt to gastrointestinal issue

iv.   You might loss excess weight.

About The Book

'Natural Supplement For Extra Man Power Booster' is a book written by Dr. Walker Sax it a 100% natural supplement and male extra manpower enhancement that was constituent with the finest herbal component that are free without fixing to boost your general sexual wellbeing and also keep you completely free from any type of erectile dysfunction.

In this book, Dr. Walker Sax also emphasize on your general body structure, physique excess body fat, fatigue, damage tissues or soreness of the bone which can also be a barrier for maintaining a better sex life.